Christ,

with Urban Fox

John F. Deane

DEDALUS

WHITE PINE PRESS

The Dedalus Press
24 The Heath, Cypress Downs, Dublin 6W. Ireland

White Pine Press
10 Village Square, Fredonia, NY 14063, U.S.A.

ISBN 1 873790 98 8 (paper) The Dedalus Press
ISBN 1 873790 99 6 (bound) The Dedalus Press

ISBN 1 877727 72 5 White Pine Press

Cover drawning by John Behan

Acknowledgments: "Something Understood", ed. Seán Dunne,
Marino 1995; *Honest Ulsterman; Agenda (U.K.); Other Poetry (U.K.);
Swarthmoor Anthology (U.K.); The Month (U.K.);The Irish Times; The
Furrow; Cyphers; Spirituality; The Literary Review (U.S.A.); Patago-
nian Winds (U.S.A.); Crab Orchard Review (U.S.A.); New Hibernia
Review (U.S.A.); Compost (U.S.A); Poesie Europe (Germany); Jungle
(France); Heat (Australia).* The poem "Father" was published in
Poetry, Chicago.
    Special thanks to Jacques Rancourt, Denise Levertov, John
Montague and Thomas Dillon Redshaw; and to the English Dept.
of Winthrop University, Rock Hill, South Carolina.

Dedalus Books are represented and distributed in the U.K. and Europe
by *Password*, 23 New Mount St., Manchester M4 4DE

Printed in Ireland by Colour Books Ltd.

The Dedalus Press receives financial assistance from
An Chomhairle Ealaíon, The Arts Council, Ireland.

The Dedalus Press

White Pine Press

─────────

CHRIST, WITH URBAN FOX

John F. Deane

CONTENTS

7   Artist
8   Kesh
9   Healer
10   Birdman
11   Cyrene
12   The Old Masters
14   The Middle Kingdom
15   No Lasting Dwelling
16   Shekinah, Old God of Tents

17   The Dream of the Rood

23   Christ, with Urban Fox
25   Drumlin Country
26   When Giants Walked
31   Swift
32   The Fox-God
33   Father
34   Out of a Walled Garden
35   Heron
36   Silence
37   Beautiful Exile
39   Heatherfield
40   What of the Night?
41   Heatherfield Downs
42   Dawn
44   At Jerpoint Abbey

45   Bunnacurry / Mala Strana
46   What's Left After Translation
47   Under the Puy de Dômes
48   Astronauts
49   Mirror-Image
50   Love-Story
51   Harbour
55   *De Mortuis . . .*
56   Building
57   Faith of Our Fathers
58   The Garden
59   The Storm

61   The Return

Artist

This was the given image –
a moulded man-body
elongated into pain, the head
sunk in abandonment : the cross;

I see it now
as the ultimate in ecstacy,
attention focused, the final words
rehearsed; there are black

nail-heads and contrasting
plashes of blood
like painter's oils : self-portrait
with grief and darkening sky;

something like Hopkins,
our intent, depressive scholar
who gnawed on the knuckle-bones of words
for sustenance – because God

scorched his bones with nearness
so that he cried with a loud voice
out of the entangling, thorny
underbrush of language.

Kesh

They sit for hours on small
fold-up canvas chairs and hunch themselves
out over their knees; absent a while; fishing;

on the water a float, red and white, jigging;

the summer cruisers at their gossiping,
at anchor off the wooden kesh, our elders
on their recliners grateful for the sun;

if you squeeze your eyes you see tiny spots
jigging against the high blue of heaven;
if you see farther you may glimpse

Jesus, appearing, disappearing, among lake-shore trees;

his footsteps clatter a moment on the boardwalk
and when you turn, anxious suddenly,
there is no one there : as if he were unsure

whether to call them from their fishing
or contemplate the perfect yellow lilies
rising from the fetid mud; he, too,

scrounging about, like the rest of us, for meaning.

Healer

They have heard tell he heals
by a simple touch or
sometimes a jerk of the bones, a
painful, liquid torsion;

they have entered his yard and have fallen
silent; like so many more
sitting on forms along the wall
who have scuffed a furrow to his back door;

they, acquainted with grief,
know of this singular man with his
large and calloused hands,
this bone-setter, healer, this exorcist;

there is coughing of cattle behind them,
slithering of hooves in the stalls;
they believe he is out there somewhere, moves
among shadows of stable and wall;

they have entered his yard and are silent
and night comes down on their distress.
The wind cuts through them like scythes.
He may have gone into his wilderness

to avoid them, distressed by human sores;
yet he knows, without their tears
he'd be only their shadow, merely their echo.
Rooks that have caterwauled in the trees

fall silent and twisted rookery shadows
dance at their feet; hen-shit on the cobbles, deep
liquid manure in the shores; to-morrow
perhaps he will come and rouse them up out of sleep.

Birdman

for John Behan

What more is to be said? he flew –
and the eyes of the world were on him.
He was master for a while,
striding down bright corridors of air
with the blackest clouds beneath him.

                    So if he looked
into the azure of God's eyes and saw
His secrets, then he had lived already
beyond fulness and his fall became
inevitable, the loving tips of God's fingers
melting his bones; his collapse

was more notorious than most men's living.

                    He had climbed high,
and now his great heart
burst in his chest, and he died,
                       died
for us men, and for our transgressions.

Cyrene

Nothing is given. Only the long delay
of affliction between now
and what is still to be. And yet –

I was following uneven paths along the way
where crowds were gathering, shiftily;
I stepped out of the sun into his
shadow; of all those loitering why was it I
who was chosen?

I hauled the rude beam for him where it weighed
mightily on my shoulder-blades and neck;
if I had wings it would have broken them
but I kept silent, swallowed down my loathing
while he walked ahead, indifferent,
suffering his own indignities.

Sometimes now when I achieve a stillness,
dusk, perhaps, smoke rising like a tree,
or noon, a cock still languidly crowing
at the sunlit limit of the village,
someone that looks like him will disappear
suddenly round the angle of a house
as if he had ever actually appeared –
the one on whom the cross of rumour has been laid –
and I feel shaken utterly

that we walk clamorously between silences
and have learned little of the scandal of the flesh.

The Old Masters

for Jack and Betty Weaver

It begins in the age
of naïvety – as if the heavens and the earth
could be held within the acreage

of just one canvas, (and on the best of days
perhaps it can or on the blackest ever
of days!) See how my new brown shoes

squeaking across the museum floor
announce my coming! I turn, embarrassed,
to Petrus Christus' *Pietà*, and there –

suddenly – I have been enticed
into a perfect landscape that thrills
with the necessity of suffering, the Christ

a legs-out fallen caricature
of the flesh as pain, the other figures
so finely balanced as though art

might compensate for the appalling lie
of the body; I am head-down legs-up involved
as Icarus was involved from the sky

down between ship and shore; (squeak-clean life
looked to its own employment while that most
naive of aspirations came to grief;)

there are children squatting on the floor
beneath the Breugel, a teacher pointing out
the simple details; one boy, bored,

big-eyed and innocent as I was, is now
watching me; for how can he care for Icarus
or his aspirations, for that head-down

legs-up involvement in the old lore
of pain, but only for the squeaking of shoes towards him
across the museum parquet floor.

The Middle Kingdom

A high rampart of rounded stones
separated salt marshland from salt sea;
to go clambering up was to take 5 steps forward

4 steps back while the world you walked on
flowed under your feet in cataracts; but then
as if newborn, you stood, and the Atlantic wind

snatched away your breathing – breakers coming
crescendo into rallentando –
and you touched on the edge of something real;

eastwards, then, the feline sea –
those estuary bubblings, shiftings, barriers
of silt and perishing things, mud-lives –

till tiding all my words there has been water,
water and the leavings of water.
Now it is the middle kingdom,

high grasses whispering, silences of the ash,
disturbing distances from either shore;
the late summer meadow is an ocean without sail,

small chittering birds are mustering to depart;
the dead – their flesh a limekiln white –
are gathering familiars round about me

and I go on building, with words, a high rampart,
– 5 steps forward 4 steps back – and am standing,
uncertain as ever, on the slow slope of a hill.

No Lasting Dwelling

He came, knocking loudly on our back door;
he brought into the kitchen a whiff of ditches
and something more we had been warned against,

some taint, ancient and enviable and unnamed;
he stood, obsequious, big-bodied, old
and took away our blackened cans, our tin mugs;

a people of unrest, they told me, feckless, shifty, lost;
their world, pitched out by the edge of ours,
was in no-man's-land, low tents, high caravans

backlit by heath and sky and mountain;
big horses grazed and famished dogs
worried at the camp's perimiters; I envied

their vanishing, how, suddenly, they were gone,
leaving our thorn bushes alight with coloured rags.
When he came back the metals gleamed again

with tiny soldering scabs where the faults had been;
he doffed his cap, winked at me, and left; I drew
in, gratefully, to the comfort of our stone hearth.

Shekinah, Old God of Tents

Like the earth we have been faithful
but now, as the country, we grow
restless; we are Bedouin, squatting in tents
at the flesh-edge of a desert – (though ours
is all within now) – dry and grainy, grit :

packing up again and moving on.
We have been witnesses to graves, and linens,
to concrete finally poured. There have been
tales and wonders, generating words
not in everyday conversation; our lives again

like sand-grains blown feverishly about.
Yet we continue faithful, like the earth
knowing invasions and migrations,
like a divided country turning uncertainly
towards the south, then towards the north.

After the first, terrible death, there have been
too many more; we set out again
seeking peace; we set out again
as often as our hope demands it, not knowing
whom we may meet along the way.

The Dream of the Rood

(a version of the 7th/8th century Anglo-Saxon poem,
often attributed to Cynewulf)

Pause with me while I tell the most precious, the best
of dreams, sent to me in the deep silence of night
when men, word mongers, were everywhere at rest.

It seemed that I saw the most marvellous tree
lifted high on the air, and all haloed in light,
most beautiful of all beams of wood; a beacon

bathed in gold; there were breathtaking gems that stood
all around the base, a further five were ablaze
high along the cross-beam. Holy angels of the Lord

looked always on its loveliness, enthralled.
This was no criminal's cross; there came to gaze
the saintliest of spirits, men everywhere and all

marvels of creation mused upon it, where it stood.
How strange that tree of victory! and I – steeped in sin,
badly blemished all over – watched that glorious wood

adorned with banners, shining in all its beauty,
garlanded in gold, glorious gems worked in –
the wonderfully wreathed tree of the World's Ruler.

Yet straight through all that gold I could still see
the friend of once-wretched men, how it first began
to bleed on the right-hand side. Sorrow bore in on me,

and fear, before that vision; I saw the beacon change,
become clothed in colours; how at times the blood ran
drenching it in blood-dew, then how it bloomed with a strange

beauty. I lay a long while, wretched at heart,
watching my Saviour's tree; until suddenly most
wonderfully, the wood spoke, uttering these words:

    "Long ago – distinctly I remember it! – one day
I was hewn down at the dark edge of the forest
and severed from my stem. Strong enemies seized me,

wrought me into a spectacle for the world to see,
commanding me to hoist their criminals on high;
men carried me on their shoulders and erected me

high on a hill – fixed there by many foes. I saw
the Ruler of mankind rush with real courage to climb
on me and I did not dare (my Lord had warned!)

bend down or break, though I saw the broad
surface of earth shiver; how simple – the Lord knows –
to smite his enemies! but firm and stout I stood,

unmoving. The hero stripped, though he was God Almighty!
robust and resolute, mounting onto the gallows
spirited, in the sight of many, to redeem mankind.

I wavered while the warrior embraced me : clasped me
and I did not dare bend down towards the ground,
fall on the earth's surface, I must stand fast.

I was raised up a Rood, carrying the powerful King,
high Lord of Heaven, and did not dare to bend.
They pierced me with bloody nails, the pain still stings!

the open wounds of malice; they made us fools
together; I was wholly wet with blood
streaming from his side when he gave up his soul

and helpless on that hill I knew a fearful fate :
stretched out in agony the Almighty God
of hosts cruelly wracked; the heavens all in spate

above the body of our Ruler, that bright radiance;
shadows reigned supreme under a thickening cloud;
all of creation mourned, moaned this cruel chance :

and Christ was on the rood.

"Now from afar came virtuous men, hastening
to that solitary Man; I saw it all, my many cares
grievously afflicting me, but I yielded to their chastening

humble and ardent hands. They held the God of Hosts,
took him down from that dreadful torture; warriors
left me wet with moisture, wounded all over by arrows,

laid him down, his limbs weary, stood watching at his head;
they looked on the Lord of heaven, resting for a time
weary from a woeful contest. A tomb was already made

in sight of those who slew him, carved out of stone,
and they laid therein our Saviour, glorious, sublime.
They began to make their songs of sorrow, they mourned

until the fall of evening, then wearily wandered home
from that royal Throne, leaving him there to rest.
We, however, a long while weeping, stood alone

on our foundations, fearing a dreadful destiny,
while that beautiful body chilled, that treasure chest
of life. Hastening then they hacked us cruelly

to the earth; planted us in a deep pit. Dark. Cold.
But the Lord's retainers, his friends, freed us, and then
set me on high, enhanced with silver and gold.

"Now, dear friend, now it is time that the world know
how I endured the wickedness of evil men
and grievous woes; it is time that the world show

honour to me through the whole earth and this broad
and marvelous creation; that they make their prayers
to me as a symbol. For on me did the Son of God

suffer agonies a while; so I won glory and was raised
high under the heavens, that I may heal the cares
of those who honour me and who offer praise;

once, I became the most terrible of tortures, of pains
most odious to men, before I opened up for them,
for these word-mongers, life's true way.

See then how the prince of Heaven honoured me beyond
all the trees of the wood, true Keeper of the Kingdom,
as he honoured his mother Mary beyond all womankind.

"Now I require you, dear friend, that you relate
what you have seen to others, reveal in words this vision:
the tree of glory on which God himself had to tolerate

suffering for the ways of men and Adam's ancient sin,
that He tasted death; that He rose truly in great
honour to give help to men, mounted high to Heaven

and will come down on judgement day, angels at His side
to judge, each man and woman in whatsoever way
they have measured out this transitory life. Nor let mankind

be unafraid of what the Ruler of the World will say!
Before the multitudes he will test, and try, to find
where is he who, for the Lord's sake, would taste

death's rancid savour as He did on the Rood?
They shall fear, for there are few who will discover
what to say to Christ that dreadfilled day. But you

who have borne on your breast this dear, divine
and best of symbols, have no fear, His blood
has won you grace over the gravit of earth for ever;

hope then, always to dwell with Him in the highest Heaven."

Oh I prayed then with courage to that happy Cross,
I was alone, no person by, knew powerful longing. My food
now is to love that tree of victory, all else is loss

and forfeiture, to honour it more often than any man yet has.
My will is directed wonderfully towards the rood.
I have no powerful friends in the world, they have passed

from the dreams of earth to the King's glory and dwell
in Heaven now with the High Father; I long
for the day when the royal Rood of the Lord shall

fetch me finally from this transitory life and bring
me where is rapture and revelry in heaven, where all
the people of the Lord shall stand and sing

at the banquet where is bliss perpetual; and I pray
that our God who suffered on the gallows tree
be my friend, who has freed us to the light of day,

the Son and victor, stalwart, successful, He
who came with a glorious consort of spirits to stay
forever within God's kingdom; that I shall see

the Almighty Ruler, risen to where the angels stand,
with the holy company of saints at God's right hand,
the hero, home with honour to his native land.

Christic, with Urban Fox

I

He was always there for our obeisance,
simple, ridiculous,
not sly, not fox, up-front – whatever
man-God, God-man, Christ – but there.
Dreadlocks almost, and girlish, a beard
trim in fashion, his feminine
fingers pointing to a perfect
heart chained round with thorns;
his closed and slim-line lips
inveigling us towards pain.

II

Did he know his future? while his blood
slicked hotly down the timbers did he know
the great hasped rock of the tomb
would open easily as a book of poems
breathing the words out? If he knew
then his affliction is charade, as is our hope;
if he was ignorant – his mind, like ours,
vibrating with upset – then his embrace of pain
is foolishness beyond thought, and there –
where we follow, clutching to the texts –
rests our trust, silent, wide-eyed, appalled.

III

I heard my child scream out
in pain on her hospital bed,
her eyes towards me where I stood
clenched in my distress;

starched sheets, night-lights, night-fevers,
soft wistful cries of pain,
long tunnel corridors down which flesh
lies livid against the bone.

IV

Look at him now, this king of beasts, grown
secretive before our bully-boy modernity,
master-shadow among night-shadows,
skulking through our wastes. I watched a fox
being tossed under car wheels, thrown like dust
and rising out of dust, howling in its agony;
this is not praise, it is obedience,
the way the moon suffers its existence,
the sky its seasons. Man-God, God-man, Christ,
suburban scavenger – he has danced
the awful dance, the blood-jig, has been strung
up as warning to us all, his snout
nudging still at the roots of intellect.

Drumlin Country

A landscape of wind-bent hedgerows,
of rushes, daub, marsh acres;
the cattle lay their bodies down
on pallets of churned mud;
the driven spade withdraws
reluctantly, soil clots and slubbers

like the soul in its long lethargy
unwilling to let go;
drains fill, the little roads
are washed into hungry rivers,
the small farms lift their heads to breathe
and the dog yaps long in hope.

It has been so for generations, names
on the headstones attest to it, proudly.
But soon this world will be forest, drumlins
suffering the slow crop for new, absentee landlords,
and the angry dead will be everywhere
blowing on the wind like spores.

When Giants Walked

Now every face but his own has vanished
from the mirror; he is the last, brown-waistcoated,
of the old generations; he must redeem his language,

renaming sounds that haunt the darkness;
his grandfather's whitened elms are ghostly shapes
but the quicks his father planted

are trees with rookeries in their brains;
sometimes he stands, secure in their protection,
to watch a star come snag on a hawthorn spike,

to feel the soft night gather him in its arms;
the gate closes behind him with an iron groan
and from his open door an old buttermilk light

falls across the yard with a soft clamour;
in the mornings the stubble on his jaws
brings another day, undifferentiated, yielding.

We are not a well-dressed people, not
dapper, having known, too long, too much
subjugation; we labour, in our wilderness,
not to re-form the world to our features

but to re-create ourselves in its likeness;
our dress takes count of God's commands
and the dictates of demanding weathers;
we have been a simple people, therefore,

tongue-tied, innocent, well-beloved.
But watch for us! we are not fools, not
primitives; we are learning subtlety, some irony;
we are joining the traffic out on the high roads

while still we tend our dead, one eye on the past,
the other on our own uncertain future.

You will hear his cough
echoing loudly amongst the sheep and cattle;
he will wrestle across the night to let

new life in through the bellowing of animals;
his trouser turn-ups cemented stiff with mud
his pleasure is to stand in a matt-wool vest,

the strain of galluses over his belly,
and watch the morning smoke out of his chimney;
he has been shepherding his dead

in small-time portraits within his missal
while he lives on in the wet valley, sharp of wit,
slooshing a living out of the long bottoms;

high on his bicycle he will sail like a ketch
down the long arterial road to the cattle mart
where he is knowledgeable, bargaining, a prince.

We have been excluded from the burnished kingdoms
where the suave and worldly-wise, well-fleshed,
dine *table d'hôte*; our lexicons are altering rapidly
to absorb new words with foreign roots;

we move awkwardly still, our hands too big,
our palates gravel-rough; our greetings, too,
hang on the air like bubbles : *Dia leat. God with you.*
Yet we, seeking truth with all our might

are still disturbed at his isolation
as if he points to the blacker edges of our mirrors,
to the darkness that is there behind us,
to the drying marrow in our bones;

he has his radio, television, phone
and unsettles us with his bonhomie, his aftershave.

*

Once there were many voices here
sounding across the air like bells;
at twelve, and six, the people stood

to bow their heads and touch their knees to the earth;
the laneways now have filled up with ghosts,
and salleys thicken through the aspen hedge;

but he stands tall, as if the world had not yet left
the stable-yard of creation; love him!
as one of the falling angels caught in middle earth,

hurt and half-believing, from forehead to navel
making the quick sign; he has been pushed,
unwittingly, into wilderness.

We have gloried in the cross of Christ so long
we have grown numb, incredulous,
– our death a living, our living death –
in a hurry now, seeking compensation

we strive for sophistication, forgetting
we are an island people, manipulated
and abandoned at the outside edge of empire;
we cradle our resentments but smear our faces

with new-age pigments. Our wild acres
nurture conifers in rows, treasure at their roots,
and silence breeding in their soft tips;
we have new festivals, new icons

but knowing always *he* hangs still above us,
his life's blood seeping, his dry mouth open.

We have created him and see! we keep him, framed,
our ringleted, long-fingered, feminine man
watching over our beds and our deal tables;

can you imagine what it was
before they came with their huge spools
and threaded us to the world?

our slow-waltz-scything in the high meadows
while the corn-crakes made the long bright night
fragile as an old delft jug? Envy us then

our certainties, when giants walked the earth
and held us in the valley of their arms.
Now the Christ, still stalking our fields in silence,

reaches hesitant hands to us out of the emptiness.

Swift

The talk is of subsidies and silage;
the new young farmers are out at dawn
valuing their days, machines –
those high-stepping, cock-tailed, grass-chewers –
leaving fields an embarrassed yellow
with plastic bales like droppings scattered round.

The swift have come again, again have learned
to master the western gales, their small hearts
working like thunder; tomorrow the hedgerows
will be battered down, and the wrens' nests
masticated into chipping offal;
we are God's breath hawed for a moment

on God's dark mirror. It seems
I have grown older, suddenly,
to be mourning the passing of things I've loved –
the monstrance held up high in golden light,
corncrakes, silences, the nice delay of Latin chant –
but my small heart still works on, like thunder.

The Fox-God

Across the fields and ditches, across the unbridgeable
mean width of darkness, a fox barked out its agony;
all night it fretted, whimpering like a famished child,

and the rain fell without pity; it chewed at its flesh,
gnawed on its bared bone, until, near dawn, it died.
The fox, they will say, is vermin, and its god

a vermin god; it will not know, poor creature,
how it is suffering – it is yourself you grieve for.
While I, being still a lover of angels, demanding

a Jacob's ladder beyond our fields, breathed
may El Shaddai console you into that darkness.
I know there was no consolation. No fox-god came.

But at dawn, man the enemy came stalking fields,
snares in his bag, a shotgun cocked. Poor
creatures. The gap out of life, we have learned,

is fenced over with affliction. We, too, some dusk,
will take a stone for pillow, we will lie down, snared,
on the uncaring earth. Poor creatures. Poor creatures.

Father

"This is the way towards kindness,"
he said, "believe me," and I did;
I saw the small brown flecks of wisdom
like rust-drops on his hands;
six blind, sleek, mewling kittens

birth-wet and innocent of claw,
he gathered into a hessian bag
with stones for travelling companions
and swung and swung it through the blue air
and out into the water of the lake.

Sometimes still I see them scrabbling,
their snout-heads raised, their bodies
nude and shivering in an alien element,
sometimes – when I see the children,
their big, wide-open eyes unseeing,

skin stretched dry and crinkling
like leather and above them the blue sky,
that enviable sun shining – again I hear
"this is the way towards kindness,
believe me" and I do, I do, I do.

Out of a Walled Garden :
Thérèse of Lisieux

I had thought of her as the insipid saint
standing demurely within her coign of dimness;
they had fenced her round with a dissonance of candles,

her habit turd-brown and curdle-cream,
her shape matrushka-soft and her eyes
squinting towards the ceiling; she held

a crucifix and plaster roses and silly women
simpered at her feet. But I have come to see
how she was an island of pain, how God enjoyed

whittling and refashioning her so she could tell
how we are breakable and mortal, how
suffering is a grace and pain a living pearl;

so they drew strength from her in Auschwitz,
they made her protrectress-saint of Russia;
what a fine explosion she would make today

rising in mushroom clouds above our world
with a fine-rain fallout of rose-red petals
misting over Chechnya and remote Pacific atolls.

Heron

It stood attentive as a carved root,
one stick-leg lifted, the splinter knife-bill
poised; yellow eye alert and all desire
focused; ashen-grey, in harmony, stilled;

I watched from the brush-bleak shore, hidden
heart (for the moment) quieted to the beast
imperatives of the world; the stab so sudden
so fast there seemed no space between

decision and execution and a small fish-body
gleamed a moment in air, was tossed and quickly
swallowed live, the passage visible
down the long neck; then, delicately

as an old woman threading a needle, it took
a high articulated step along the world; only in me
the shuddering, my mind already turning back
to dreaming, angers, disillusion, fears.

Silence

I was watching for the flight past
of a comet that would not pass again
in over a thousand years; I saw

only the stars and once the steady
unremarkable progress of some
man-made scrap-heap drifting across the sky;

but I was satisfied, awed once more
by the unaccountable night.
Somewhere in earth-darkness a dog

barked and fell silent; I inhaled
stars and quiet and my own minuscule standing
on the rim of the world, how the silence

that stretched before the music of the spheres
would have been an orchestra tuning up,
a strife of instruments before the symphony's great

knock-on-the-door, or how the prolonged
vegetable and animal quiet utterly failed
when a human voice screamed from behind a hill.

Beautiful Exile

Reynolds
watched old mosses grow back in cracks between the
paving-stones, saw slugs invade the sewer-pipes and
leave their shimmering tracks along the kitchen tiles,

watched
Jonathan's wife in seventeen the Mews loosen her blouse
in the back garden for what was there else to do? Jonathan in the city, labouring in the high square buildings
made of green glass tiles,

Jonathan's wife
naked behind the garden wall rubbing the dark moist
soil against her flesh as if mourning the tubers that had
rotted there in an earlier famine;

beautiful
exile, Reynolds breathed, but she heard him and
screamed, fearing the black stubble on his face, the list-
less fall of the stalks of his hair, the black moist soil
thickening under his finger-nails.

Sometimes Reynolds
heard the earth exhale under its weight of suburbs,
sometimes he heard the winds make passionate forest-
music across the chimneys and satellite dishes,

sometimess he saw
the old thick-bearded dumb-with-anger unfashionable
God go dance like a crazy about the balls and crooklocks
of the new wrought-iron gates;

they have planted
rubble, Reynolds thought, a bare six inches below the
soil, defeated, disgruntled rubble and some day it will
have grown so high as to overwhelm them all in their
places.

If he could say it – just once –
to Jonathan's wife perhaps she would come to him and
he could bury his tear-dry face in the moist soil of her
flesh.

Heatherfield

The tall stiff snow-drops of the street-lights
blossom on through the suburban winter chill;
the lawns are hard as patios; overnight
great herds of cars, stalled, lie primed and still
and will rise again, steaming, after dawn;
houses cast their shadows over houses, bald,
stolid as crop-headed young philosophers who draw
eyelids down against unseemly cold;
after mid-morning mass, the elderly
gather in small surviving groups
and words fly up in clouds over their heads
like doves of hope; they clap their hands repeatedly
to applaud their living still; and what is left to do?
we shiver in this last, demanding, wilderness.

What of the Night?

Three shapes,
actual and reified, detached themselves from the mias-
mic orange light under the suburb-lamps, climbed the
wall from Heatherfield Avenue and spotted the BMW;

Reynolds
heard a hacksaw against the lock on suave-faced Jackson's gate, setting Reynolds's teeth ablaze;

they wrenched wide
the car door, setting the light alert in Jackson's window,
bringing Jackson's shattered face to the glass;

warriors,
intoxicated by violence, waltzed in the driveway, the car
making scrape-music along the twisted iron of the gate,
humming down Heatherfield Drive and away into a
definitely circumscribed future;

came Jackson,
pyjamaed, to his door, urgent to dispense violence, a
carving-knife in his hand, Jackson, actual and reified,

and Reynolds
sighed for the innocence of a black night, with stars
visible, the rustling sounds of predators and their vic-
tims audible and whispering till the answer would come
clear as an angelus bell,

all is well, Reynolds, yes, all is well.

Heatherfield Downs

We live in a languid ordering of bricks
accommodating citizen cat and
upwardly mobile magpie, we boast
palm trees of washing in our small back yards.
Do not deny us goals : watch
the shoaling of our lives each morning
out onto the great river of the world;
then in the evening we are small yachts
breezing into port, names on our houses :
"Haven", "Mountain View", "Marbella".
Down these dim-lit wards our sleep is brittle
but there is shelter here from the easterlies,
there are dreams and the same ongoing search,
frantic sometimes as yours, for happiness.

Dawn

I came out into pre-dawn darkness;
a fine rain was falling through the amber
aura of the street-lamps;

here in the suburbs we expect no cock-crow,
lights will come on in bath- or bed-room, lives
plugged in again, switched on;

the rubbish has been set out, uncertain
sentinel at each front-garden wall;
we were beginning to suspect an interloper –

black plastic sacks ripped open identifying
a brute invisible hunger, some real presence
disturbing to us. I stood awhile, perplexed;

this is not how I had envisaged it, these
sedulous rows of houses, tarmacadam lawns,
as if the words I'd learnt had slewed away

from what they named, the way my flesh
has lost intercourse with the hard earth;

and then I saw it, beautiful beast body

slipping like memory across unsociable darkness;
"fox", I whispered, "fox";
it saw me, too, we touched a moment

until it turned, disdainfully, and I heard the soft
pat pat pat on the concrete of its proud withdrawal
down the street, around a corner;   it disappeared

and left me thrilling, as if to name it were enough
to have everything back in place, the hedgerows,
immanence, survival, the eternal laws.

At Jerpoint Abbey

for Tony and Jane O'Malley

We have dropped ruins of our faith
like coins out of our pockets; we come
poking for mystery and that wholeheartedness
once binding nave to chancel; this Abbey

was austere, Cistercian, on its tombs
a pride of saints, of floriated croziers
and knights in mail; I see the monks
in black and white about the cloister garth

ambulating into God's good graces;
no fools, they carved onto their columns
bishops lords and ladies lest they underestimate
the body's benefactors; every life

resists being purged of the soft bark of self.
Did they cry out, I wonder, as the jackdaws cry,
did they prey on one another, as we prey?
The cock-eyed wagtails rule where I go drifting

among tourists, gargoyles and grotesques,
aware our God's more functional, more prosaic,
as if the stone had been rolled home (the angels
fled) and mercenaries had been venturing back.

Bunnacurry, Achill Island /
Mala Strana, Prague

I was alone in the big dark bedroom, scared;
on the mantelshelf our little golem-god
with the orb in his hand as if he were terrified

it might break; I breathed into the space
where conspiring spirits lurked :
O holy Child Jesus of Prague – pray for us.

Can holy God ever have been a child?
Once I masturbated in the dusk and
found him watching out of accusing silence;

I swept him from the mantel to the hard floor
but he went on presiding, with head askew.
The people shook their fists at tanks in Prague

where he disappointed me again,
ornate, isosceles triangle doll, while we,
caricatures of ourselves, step back

manipulating cameras and the solitary heart;
on Charles bridge a child is begging, the people
toss her coins and I think of all the children

of Biafra, Ethiopia, Ireland, Dunblane;
I am alone again in the big bedroom, scared;
can holy God ever, ever have been a child?

What's Left after Translation

(trouvé on a bedside table, Prague)

The guest is obtained especially

to behave himself to not give rise to a fire –
to come throw the hanged fire-alarming
instruction and the accommodation rule –
to get acquainted with the dislocation
of the handle extinguisher –

not to smoke and manipulate with open fire
on the dangerous place –
to keep the prohibition of the using of private
non-filed and non-permitted electrical appliances –
to keep the prohibition of a disassembly
of protective covers and other irregularities
and doing unprofessional interventions
and to be announced to the reception.

In the case of the rise of a fire
the guest is obtained especially
to act after the directions disposed
in the fire-alarming directions –
to notice and be obtained that
mobile extinguishers are at disposal
for the liquidation of a fire rising.

And all peace and restful willy to the guest.

Under the Puy de Dômes

for Patricia and Richard Martineau

So this is the wide new world? I was born
on an island off an island off an island
off the western limits of Europe
and was brought up to believe
in a God of love, crucified.

Like a pilgrim I have toiled
up the long slope, been offered glimpses
of snow-pine peaks above the city's roofs
and beyond, a welcoming, tangerine sky.
I have clambered down into a crypt

with everywhere the small brass plaques
saying *Danke. Merci. Gracias;*
there are abandoned crutches, bandages,
the rosaries and medals speaking that old
language I heard round our holy wells :

– the world, they say, is a stained-glass window
wonderfully shattered – while in a niche
half-darkling the Virgin still gives suck
to the old child, and see! under soft
lighting, our islandman, hanging, crucified!

Astronauts

They are tinfoil crayfish in free drift
through the underwater world of space;
they walk nonchalantly out on emptiness,
balance on fingertips a factory of steel;

what we miss are the bubbles
rising reassuringly above them and
tying them still to our breathing;
words emanate from them like the words we spoke

in childhood into resonating old tin cans;
further space is black beyond black
and the earth looms bigger and more beautiful
than we had remembered;

ah well, perhaps they will have learned something
and will come back to tell us if they can find the words.
Sometimes this is how I see it – death –
and I am turning slowly in an old-time waltz

outwards, away from camera, in silence;
I am a lexicon dispersed, debris
among debris or even, for a moment,
a shooting star in somebody's night sky.

Mirror-Image

My God, in his self-regarding, took
me up in an embrace of love and
dashed me against a stone wall.
I heard the rending of metals, felt
the grinding of steel but I suffered
not even a kiss on my soft flesh.
I got out and stood in a chrome silence.

Often since then I have watched them
gather me off the road, the shattered
spectacles, the flitches of bone and gum;
I have no wish to lie naked to naked
clay but feel guilty, as if I've rejected
a gesture of love. As if I had drawn down
thick curtains between His face and me.

Love-Story

Poor Clares. Poor
Clares : cloistered
for centuries from our eyes
they nurtured the flowerhead of affliction;

our boisterous age has foisted
new economies on them and we bring
our coughs and raincoats, our tousled nights
into their morning;

they have admitted us
into their forecourt; see how they move
shoft-shoed across perfect floors
as if they have already died

and are waiting . . .
Their high-pitched, sweet
old-woman voices tremble like doves
under the ceiling; here

the body comfortable, the mind
at ease, they have been caught in the quicklime
and erosion of their Christ;
what a fine old love-story it has been,

drawing to its close now, into
its consummation. We
have located ourselves a moment
in their space; the day

is ahead of us, the cars
waiting; soon we will move,
congratulating one another,
back to our own affairs.

Harbour

A garden, langueur of sunshine, mid-morning;
distant, subdued sea-sounds; I am there, not there,
involved and not involved; mother on a deck-chair

self-absorbed; a dog lies indolent; perhaps I play
with buttercups, daisies, building blocks . . .
The woman turns suddenly, as if someone

said her name; she shivers, smiles at me and says
"someone has stepped over my grave". Haunting
me still, with its pointlessness, its surf-sounds.

I was crouched over the water, absorbed,
floating a stick, bone-white, knuckle-ended,
that would not sink in the drain's maelstrom;

I was part of the turning world, obedient,
it was another time, child of that time
I do not praise it. God

was sea-water about the islands,
sounding every thought; I left, my pockets weighted
with the coins of old obsessions.

Sometimes you'd like a poem that holds it all
if only the words stopped slipping through.
These days, back on the island, I seem

to be walking in an altered landscape, the sea
smashing against the shore, renaming it;
I stand and listen to its chant, the plainsong

of longing in the air, as of old monks
crazed with loneliness whose psalms
were a rope mooring desire to God,

male voices, seeking repose and gravity; You
have formed me out of ocean-water, they sang,
in Your image, my dust is salt, my living thirst.

Sometimes you'd like a poem to hold it all,
like illumined books that wash the words
in meadow-flowers and sea-monsters.

We lay on rugs at the strand's edge;
I was small yet, burrowing into awareness,
bucket and spade before me, building;

desire was a seed
plumping itself in darkness; father
was in the waves, swimming, my spade

beating on the pink splat of a jellyfish;
granny sat on a deck-chair, in black as always,
mother, breast-down on a rug, reading the world news;

this is the moment that I started from, the moment
I come back to, here where the sea has taken
granny, mother, father

away into its keeping; guilty almost, that father
did not call for help, was drawn by currents
out of our reckoning into the dark.

I had a spinning top, and on it scarlet soldiers
beat on yellow drums and marched on a green field;
I pumped and pumped until it hummed,

pumping against the sounds from the room upstairs,
words for the dying, the voices murmuring
like bees in summer searching sweetness;

the old man's face was wax,
malleable gold; soon there was silence;
somebody closed the dead man's eyes, joined his hands;

there was a different murmur in the room, a small
bustling, an evening stillness; he lived long –
they soothed themselves – he died well.

The island graveyard is all cross and headstone,
sea-shell patterning, slant of plot and walkway,
harbour, alyscamps, the fullness of desire.

I stand alone a while, listening;
the grasses have taken over, and the wild flowers;
all that remains is profound silence.

After the night's storm
women stand in groups along the pier, waiting;
they speak quietly; they have sipped tea;

word will come, or not; they are open, waiting.
In the small harbour a blue shark floats
brushing against the walls, its off-white belly

bloated; soon, a fullness, but not still, the trawlers
hoisted where they loll, one space
vacant; riffles of sea-breeze over the water;

widows already, waiting;
lives that have been filled with yearning
have been dulled at last

after the long patience, one hand
to the mouth, troubled, language at a loss,
only the wind speaking, the sea-wind.

Deep calling to deep, across great emptiness.

De Mortuis . . .

We spoke fondly of the dead tonight
drawn together round an open fire;
out in the shadows I could sense them

doing their soft-shoe shuffle, we and they
content with one another for a while;
but they keep on slipping from our hold

down portrait-darkened corridors,
they disappear through walls
instants before they can be questioned

though we pray them stop!
Are they, then, restless as we are? discontent
with words like *death, nostalgia, heaven, hell* . . .

Sometimes I grow irritable with them, I hear
their malevolent tongues clacking in my head;
they are with God, may whisper to his heart

the needs of our ongoing autonomy and do not;
though we speak fondly of the dead tonight
we stay more surely speechless with unknowing.

Building

Here, in black and white, the dragging
of desire; he stands, holding the child high

like a trophy; she, beside him, smiles
indulgently; a telegraph pole in the background

sings possibilities, you can imagine
the music, the sea-saw sitting of swallows;

in his eyes the new stone shed
he has begun to build, the hen-run, plans

for field and meadow; his hands are fidgeting
for labour, his tie is already undone.

In rubble now around the old red house
the falls of plaster and shattered slates;

he has vanished from the frame, too young and
almost before the swallows; but his eyes watch

from the stones, moist with yearning, to tell
how a life goes on reaching, reaching, reaching . . .

Faith of Our Fathers

You have surrounded us for centuries
with your love; why, then, have our hearts
so rarely beaten high with joy?

you have ruminated absently
while our famine bodies filed in silence
to your altar-rocks, we have been

true to you, true till death;
we have revered them, the fathers, those
knuckle-breasted lovers of bitterness

who had not yet ascended from the catacombs;
your generals have made opaque for us
the bright windows of reason; so now take care!

we have begun to hate you, we are about
to turn to lesser gods who will not love us
with such gravity, such devotion.

The Garden

Beyond the high window the garden is in bloom;
there is an old woman moving with her secateurs;
she has carried the face of Christ on her heart
and worn a scarf always against her gift of hair;

now is the afternoon lethargy of pain;
down in the drawing-room a child, bored,
riffles piano keys; the woman stands confused :
if she could have gathered it all up into words

or once have formulated the perfect prayer
she might have learned the quieting of the soul.
This day's dust is settling down between the joists,
veronica droops in a cut-glass bowl;

her face, from the oval bevelled mirror,
looks out at her with a sorry century's dearth;
soon she too will have sighed back into Christ,
desire stilled in the black flesh of the earth.

The Storm

You have been too long absent;
we have been drifting on a violent ocean
while our children dig our hearts out
with their indifferent, probing, fingernails;

you have been too long silent; we have thought
to go down into the wilderness of sand
to take our place among the beasts
and unsouled things, to know at least

their peace; I drift on a violent ocean,
the one I love drifts with me, my eyes
are turned on her and hers on me until –

at times – I have been willing to believe
absence and silence are the oars to grasp
till you come, chiding, striding on the waters.

The Return

to Ursula

I

These are the Carolina boulevards,
these are the cities built
for cars.

I have been walking for hours, solitary,
only my own deluded footsteps
cluttering behind me.

There are copperheads among the grasses,
mosquitoes, scorpions,
raccoon, cotton-plants, mocking-birds . . .

the confusing paradise of childhood and
in its belly, the slimed
uncoiling serpent of necessity.

*

I had been down to the gate as usual, watching;
in the hedge some dust-life stirred –
sparrow, field-mouse, rat;

he's just late, I said, but mother's frame
gathered a frightening rigidity; she busied herself
a certain distance from the phone; the house

braced itself, attentive, as if the surge of happening
could somehow be restrained;
when the news broke, it brought the bustle of relief,

anger released like spray, the long outbreathing
already begun to shore away into the past,
leaving the man's words hollow, his grip unsure.

II

I have been walking on the tracks, stepping
from sleeper to sleeper, counting days – tracks
in a long sweep running
between Philadelphia and Tampa,

through Baltimore, St. Petersburg, and Raleigh.
How the rails gleam, ahead, behind me;
I lay my head to the iron and hear –
not angels on Jacob's ladder ascending and descending –

only my own heart hurting and the Carolina breeze
brushing tree-tops into sea-sounds,
waves gentle along the sands, those summers
when all manner of things seemed well.

*

All night I could hear it — after the day's
schooling — soothing, the sea,
like the whispering of winds across the pines
with their offered shelter; father was by,

his partridge stance, and mother,
her encompassing wings;
after the self-accusing rituals that placed me
in a wilderness of sins, for I had map

and chart and compass long before
I knew the journey, that we were fallen,
that the pines would stand too soon
shivering and scrawny like plucked fowl.

III

Wires hummed above us, making the world one.
If you put your ear to the creosote poles
you could imagine the high buzz of

Chinese, Yankee, French;
sometimes the winds that riddled in from the Atlantic
raised high-pitched, sliding fiddle-tunes

along the wires till you could think the air
an intricate score of world-music
hummed by a pottering God; with a good aim

you could ping a stone off the cups and send
clay chips flying everywhere
like pattern plates smashed to jigsaw fragments.

*

Such a small island,
remote, enclosed,
my people old as oracles,

diffident, true
but sending their sons and daughters out
into the big world, earning.

Now it is Fall, and I am hanging
high above the Blue Ridge
ocean of mountains, rust-orange, dust-lemon,

I am crossing – Virginia to
Kentucky – floating on a soundless
score of ghost-lives, dead words.

IV

Granny was big and mothering,

wore off-white corsets and soft blacks.
Her thin grey hair seemed soiled suds
gathered in a net; but she darned my grey socks
with purple wool, my white vests daffodil yellow.

I wonder how she saw me, in some
brightly-coloured future? or as if, with love,
you could sunder things and put them again together?
I see her, always, unravelling into grey and white.

Grandfather said the universe

was ordered as his workshop was :
angles, T-squares, the mathematical necessities.
Along the walls hung rows of cartridge belts
with all the tools in constabulary order;

on the kitchen mantelpiece he kept his pipes;
I watched him rub fragrant plug between the heels
of his palms, fill it in, and pack it down
and clouds of smoke went drifting on a perfect sky.

When he died she had a grave-space kept

beside him, this final double bed conceived
with a quilt of marble chippings; the stone
had space for her name, too; the plantain
grew up between the chip-stones, tiny lichens

spread age-flecks across the stone's face; she died
two hundred miles away, obedient still
to the world's ways, and was laid down
in a narrow suburban bed among strangers.

V

Dublin, when I left, slept in a fug
of pre-dawn light; you were standing at the door
under the pale street-lamp, your right hand

lifted in farewell; mine
an unreal adventure, bag filled with poems
carrying their freight of an island being

needing assurance; Aer Lingus, Sabena, Delta –
the demands of take-off.
Dublin. New York. Buffalo.

*

There was a many-coloured chart of Ireland
on the school-room wall, and another smaller one
of the whole world; I was alert and waiting,

I had my slate, my chalk, my duster,
the smell of new books, abundance of time;
it was beginning, all was well. Attend.

I held my hand out; the rhododendron wand,
fell heavily;
                    but I cried
with the numbness of failure,

my readable, verified world had bucked
and left me vulnerable and ashamed;
back at my desk I looked again – the words

were as I had said them, Jacob slept
with stones under his head and was recompensed
with a vision of the angels;

I raised my hand, to explain merely, to restore
wholeness.
                    He came at me
cuffing the words down into silence.

VI

Cambridge; and Harvard Yard;

the bulk carriers of learning; on the patios
swing saffron-coloured pumpkins
shaped to the inane grin

of the incomprehensible dead with which
we mock ourselves, remembering
the birds of paradise and our total fall;

the feet of scholars make brittle sounds
through the fallen leaves – "and what is man"
they say "that thou art mindful of him?"

VII

Did you learn anything in school today? — Oh yes :
the sting of a rhododendron switch across the palm,
the scalding hang of the grub-flesh of a boy

who sat on my chest and threatened me with his piss,
the sing-song old-time rhythms of the poetry of God,
the distance and disaster of the otherness of girls;

you begin in error, not in ignorance, he said,
till sin is beaten out of you; attend.
I sat in a nether desk where I indulged

the secretive, secreting imagination :
girl-illusions, patterns of autonomy, the word.
I watched the priests in their black ranks

draw woe and wrath to one another
over the congregation like a cross-saw;
the Jesuits – must-smell, sweet mints, wings

useless for flight, bringing their militant,
old-Spanish wisdom – elements, rudiments, grammar –
down with the pandy-bat on our hardening hands;

once I had been bare-arsed, constrained
over the foot of the bed while the man stroked
hard against my flesh with the bitter strap

in the name of the Father and of learning; I learned
to skulk about the grounds, use words
like jacks and homo, pass dirty pictures round.

VIII

Pleasant Street, Cincinnati;
where Germans came, reaching to create
another Rhineland, vineyards cascading down the hills,

new hope growing in dark, plumped clusters;
now there is only the low and louring
half-boarded housing, with figures shifting

through spectral light; I fear them,
their lounging, the balaclavas, the sudden
violence erupting from their bones; men

become shadows, night-creatures, those
prowling non-things that terrorized my nights.
Where are you here, old God, rueful, strict, refined?

IX

I spent such years
striving to sheen my life to a glass
where God could admire his countenance;

I was one of that tardy generation
who dressed ourselves in black and were left
standing on a wet ledge when the earth shifted;

the hours we chanted, standing in rows
like cormorants on a wind-blown shore
shivering together, though at night we could

lay ourselves down in the darkness of obedience;
it was decreation, unlearning, while the world
skipped briskly by our windows.

*

I stood, in surplice, above her grave;
I was back, suddenly, on the island and she
humming, poured paraffin in the blood-lamp

before the crude, dead Heart; we buried her, almost
anonymous, in the new suburbs and I turned away
knowing myself more lonely now than she was.

X

I have heard too much today
my own voice circling
my own concerns;

where I am now darkness
offers cacophony of insects, like
softly-blown whistles, like

disharmony of tele-signals;
you are five hours and three
thousand miles from me,

you have been asleep for hours;
I would penetrate your dreams
to say I love you

and that I miss you
terribly; above –
through leaves of the pecan-tree –

the patient answering of stars
to God's insistences;
you might turn in your sleep

distantly disturbed by the sounds
of my thoughts of you; I listen
to the sphere-music of your dreams,

of the stars and branches and night-insects,
and feeling true again, and small,
I may yet sleep dreamingly.

XI

Atlanta, Gerogia; we lift into the night;
Richmond, Washington, New York, Portland, Halifax . . .
all the instruments speak

return.
This, then, is what I have come to –
a small suburban house,

an inch of soil over builders' rubble;
frustrated terriers yap about our walls
and errand-boys push endless messages of loss

through our brass letter-box;
no blazing fire and yet no gloom
deepening to darkness;

below me the Atlantic glimmers at last
in dawn light and there! on the horizon
Ireland. You will be waiting, your hands

lifted in welcome;
I will drop my bags to embrace you.
My heart will be healed again of the old wounds.